The Sun, the Moon, and the Stars

Can there be life on other planets?
What is a "black hole"?
Is the sun burning up?
What makes the moon shine?
How big is outer space?

These are just a few of the exciting questions that are answered in *The Sun, the Moon, and the Stars.* Newly revised and updated, this easy-to-read introduction to astronomy gives the latest facts about our universe.

Dr. Ira Freeman was Professor of Physics at Rutgers University and is now a consulting physicist. He and his wife, Mae Freeman, a science educator, have written many popular science books for boys and girls.

The Sun,
the Moon,
and the Stars

Revised Edition

by Mae and Ira Freeman

illustrated by René Martin

Random House New York

Copyright © 1959, 1979 by Mae and Ira Freeman
New illustrations copyright © 1979 by Random House, Inc.

All rights reserved under International and Pan-American Copyright Conventions.
Published in the United States by Random House, Inc., New York, and simultaneously in Canada by
Random House of Canada Limited, Toronto.

Library of Congress Cataloging in Publication Data

Freeman, Mae Blacker.
  The Sun, the Moon, and the Stars.

  SUMMARY: An introduction to astronomy covering the solar system, galaxy, universe, and the latest
theories about quasars, pulsars, and black holes.
  1. Astronomy—Juvenile literature. [1. Astronomy] I. Freeman, Ira Maximilian, joint author. II. Martin,
René, fl. 1965- III. Title.
QB46.F78 1979   520   78-64604
ISBN 0-394-80110-5   .   .
ISBN 0-394-90110-X lib. bdg.

Cover illustrations: Patricia Wynne

Illustrations on pages 4, 11, 15, 19, 30, 45, and 55: W. T. Mars

Manufactured in the United States of America   9 0

Contents

The World You Know

You live on the earth. It is your world, and you know it very well. You can see its lakes, rivers, and mountains. You can see its farms and forests, its small towns and big cities. All over your world, trucks and trains and ships and planes move around from one place to another.

But from far away you cannot see any of these things. To an astronaut out in space, the earth looks like a huge colored ball. The waters of the oceans are dark blue. The clouds look like white streaks. Land shows up as brown patches.

The earth is very, very old. At first, it was only a soft lump of hot, melted rock. Slowly it began to cool off and harden. The lump took the shape of a ball, with a hard outside crust. Then, much later, water and air formed. The water steamed and bubbled. It ran into all the low places and became the oceans. At last soil formed, and plants began to grow.

All this took a long, long time. It took millions and millions of years for the melted rock to become the earth—the place you know so well.

From out in space, the earth looks like a huge ball.

The Earth Turns

The earth is always turning. But you do not notice the turning because everything stays in place on the earth as it goes around. You stay in place. Houses and trees stay in place. Even the layer of air that covers the earth stays in place.

Things do not float off the turning earth into space. That is because the earth pulls everything to itself. This pull is called gravity.

Everything that is near the earth is pulled to it by gravity. Here are some ways to see what gravity does. Throw a ball into the air. It comes right down again. Gravity pulls it down. Jump off a chair. Gravity pulls you down and makes you land quickly on the floor.

The engines of a plane work to keep it up in the air. If they are shut off, gravity pulls the plane down.

The engines must work to keep an airplane up.

Sunlight on the Earth

In the daytime, the sun shines in a blue sky. You can see everything around you, bright and clear. But at night the sky is dark, and things outdoors look

dim and shadowy. In the sky, you can see only the twinkling stars and sometimes a pale moon.

Day and night come, one after the other, because the earth keeps turning. You can find out for yourself how this happens. Get a soft rubber ball, a flashlight, and a knitting needle. Stick the knitting needle through the middle of the ball.

Sunshine and then darkness come to every place on earth.

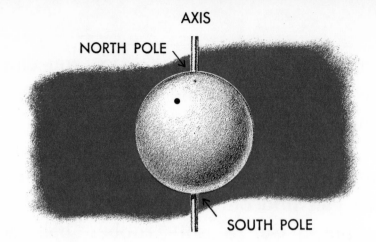

Mark a dot on the ball. Pretend the ball is the earth, the flashlight is the sun, and the dot is where you live.

The place where the knitting needle sticks out on top is the North Pole. The place where it sticks out at the bottom is the South Pole. The line that the knitting needle makes through the center of the ball is called the axis.

Pull the shades down to darken the room. Then switch on the flashlight and lay it on the table. Let the light shine on the ball as you turn it slowly around its axis. The picture on the next page shows how to do it. See how the dot comes around into the light. That means it is morning there.

As you keep turning the ball, the dot moves through the light part for daytime. When the dot goes into the dark part, it means that the sun has set and night has started. Around through the dark goes the dot until it comes out into the light. Then it is morning again. As the earth keeps going around, each place gets its turn to come into the sunshine for day and then into the darkness for night.

The turning of the earth brings night and day.

The Earth Moves Through Space

The earth moves along through space while it turns. Use your earth-ball to show this. Hold it at both ends of the axis and keep turning it as you walk across the room. The ball turns and moves along at the same time.

Where does the earth go as it moves along? It travels in a huge circle around the sun. This path around the sun is called the earth's orbit.

Each full turn of the earth on its axis takes one day.

Each full orbit around the sun takes one year.

The earth's axis is not straight up and down. It is slanted a little to one side. And the slant stays the same while the earth moves along its orbit.

The part of the earth that leans toward the sun gets more direct sunlight. Also, it stays longer in the sunlight. That means it is summer there.

The part of the earth that leans away from the sun has weaker sunlight and shorter days. It is winter there.

That is how the tilt of the earth's axis gives us the different seasons. That is why we have summer, fall, winter, and spring.

As the slanted earth travels around the sun, the seasons change.

What the Sun Does for Us

The earth needs the sun. It gives us light. It gives us heat. We could not live without the sun and the things we get from sunlight.

Sunlight makes plants grow. From plants we get most of our food. Plants give us cotton for making clothes and wood for building houses.

Plants that grew a very long time ago turned into coal and oil. We use these for heating our houses. Oil gives us the fuel that runs cars, trucks, planes, and ships.

Scientists can change oil and coal into wonderful kinds of medicine, dyes, plastics, and cloth.

The sunshine that comes to our earth gives us all these things and many more.

Sunlight warms the air. The warmed air goes up. Then cool air moves in from all around. This moving air is the wind.

The sun warms the oceans and lakes and rivers. It makes them give up some of their water. The water goes up into the air to form clouds. Later, it falls as rain or snow.

Try to imagine the earth without sunlight. The stars would shine in a black, black sky all the time. Everything would be frozen hard, even the air! There would be no life of any kind on earth. No animals at all, not even insects. No plants or trees. And, of course, no people.

Sunlight makes the air move.

The Moon

On a night when the moon is up, its soft light lets you see the shapes of trees and houses. Sometimes moonlight is strong enough to make shadows on the ground.

But when the moon is not up, it is very dark outdoors. In the country, far away from any street lights, it is hard to see anything at all.

Light from the moon is not nearly as strong as the blazing light of the sun. That is because the moon has no light of its own to shine down on the earth. The moon can only catch light from the faraway sun and throw some of it toward the earth. Light that bounces off something in this way is called reflected light. The moon reflects only a tiny bit of sunlight to the earth.

The moon is a ball, like the earth. But there are times when it does not look like a ball at all.

Sometimes you see the whole moon lit up by the sun. Then it looks round:

Sometimes you see the moon lit up only on one side. Then it looks like this:

Sometimes only a little part of the moon catches the sunshine:

The moon moves in an orbit around the earth. It takes almost one month to make each trip.

The earth's gravity pulls the moon and keeps it from going off into space. You can see for yourself how gravity does this.

The earth's gravity pulls the moon.

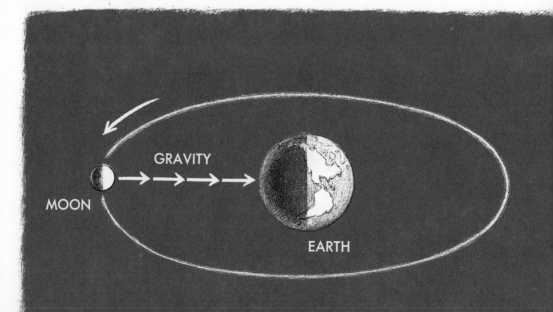

MOON

GRAVITY

EARTH

Make a hole through the middle of a small raw potato. Put a long string through the hole, and tie it tightly. Hold the other end of the string, and swing the potato around in a circle high over your head. You will feel the strong pull of the string.

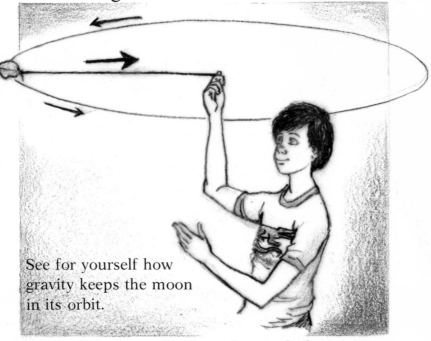

See for yourself how gravity keeps the moon in its orbit.

Your hand is the earth, and the potato is the moon. The pull of the string is the pull of gravity. This pull makes the moon stay in its orbit as it goes around and around the earth.

The moon is really about 2,000 miles (3,200 kilometers) wide. But it seems small when you see it high in the sky. That is because it is so far away. It takes a spacecraft more than two days to go from the earth to the moon.

Astronauts who visit the moon find it very different from the earth. There is no air. There is no water. In the sunshine, it is as hot as the inside of a baking oven. But in the shade, it is colder than dry ice.

The moon has high, sharp mountain peaks. The ground is sandy, and some of it is covered with gray dust. Everywhere, there are round holes in the ground. The holes are called craters. Some of the craters are as small as a soup bowl. Some are so big it would take half a day to drive around the rim.

There are many craters on the moon.

The Family of the Sun

The earth is not alone in space. It belongs to a family called the solar system. The head of this family is the sun.

The main members of the sun's family are the planets. Each one has a name. They are Mercury, Venus, Earth, Mars, Jupiter, Saturn, Uranus, Neptune, and Pluto. Pluto is the smallest planet, and Jupiter is the biggest. Earth is one of the smaller planets.

Look up at the sky on a clear night. You will see many stars. Most of them look like tiny dots that twinkle and sparkle. But on some nights you will

22   Earth is one of the smaller planets.

PLUTO

MERCURY

MARS

VENUS

URANUS

EARTH

NEPTUNE

SUN

SATURN

JUPITER

find one or two dots that seem bigger and brighter than the others. They shine with a steady light and do not twinkle. These are planets.

The planets do not give off light of their own. They only reflect some of the sunlight that shines on them.

The planets all belong to the same family because they all go around the sun. Each one moves in its own orbit. The orbits of some planets are quite close to the sun. Some are very far away.

The sun has gravity, just as the earth does. The pull of the sun's gravity keeps the planets from wandering away into space.

Look at the drawing on pages 26-27 to see the orbits of the planets. Some planets are too far away from the sun to get much light and heat from it. Some are so near the sun that the heat is like fire.

Scientists are not sure that there is life

on any planet except our own. The orbit of the earth seems just right for us. The earth gets the amount of light and heat from the sun that all living things need.

What do you mean when you say, "Far away?" How far away are things on earth? The next town may be 10 miles (16 kilometers) away. Another big city may be 100 miles (160 kilometers) away. You may have to travel 1,000 miles (1,600 kilometers) to get to another country.

But even 1,000 miles is a very tiny distance when you talk about outer space. The earth is nearly 100 million miles (160 million kilometers) from the sun. And some of the other planets are much, much farther away from the sun.

Suppose you start out from the sun on the very day you are born. You travel in a fast spaceship that never stops.

You will be 4 months old before you cross the orbit of Mercury.

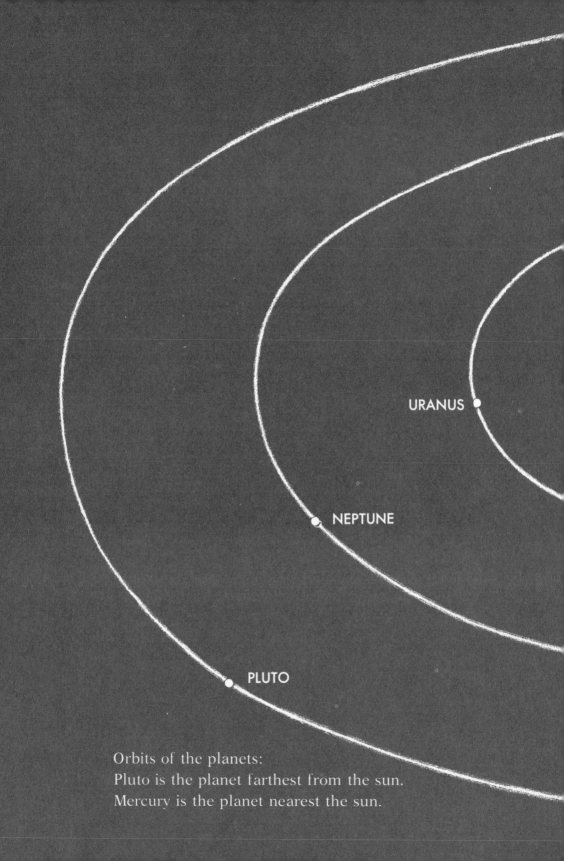

URANUS

NEPTUNE

PLUTO

Orbits of the planets:
Pluto is the planet farthest from the sun.
Mercury is the planet nearest the sun.

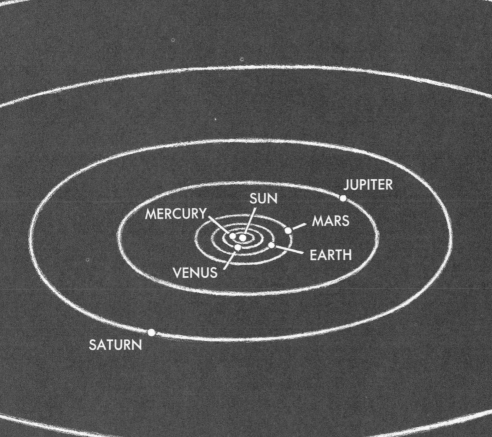

JUPITER

SUN

MERCURY

MARS

EARTH

VENUS

SATURN

27

You will be 7 months old when you cross the orbit of Venus.

You will be over 10 months old when you cross the orbit of your own earth.

You will be more than a year old when you cross the orbit of Mars.

You will be almost old enough for kindergarten when you cross the orbit of Jupiter.

You will be over 8 years old when you cross the orbit of Saturn.

You will be a high school senior when you cross the orbit of Uranus.

You will be 26 years old when you cross the orbit of Neptune.

At last you cross the orbit of the planet that is farthest out from the sun—Pluto. And you will be 34 years old. That is how long it takes to make the trip, traveling in a fast spaceship.

More About the Planets

MERCURY is the planet nearest the sun. It is less than half as wide as the earth. Mercury takes about 3 months to travel around the sun. The sunny side of Mercury is hotter than an oven. The side away from the sun is colder than anywhere on earth. Mercury has no moons.

VENUS is the brightest planet in the sky. It is a little smaller than the earth and is our nearest planet neighbor. Venus takes about $7\frac{1}{2}$ months to go around the sun. This planet is covered by heavy clouds that trap the heat. Venus is even hotter than Mercury. Venus has no moons.

EARTH is our own planet. It is a little less than 8,000 miles (13,000 kilometers) wide. Our planet takes one year to go around the sun. Many kinds of plants and animals can live on earth because it is not too hot or too cold. Earth has one moon about 2,000 miles (3,200 kilometers) wide.

MARS is about half as wide as the earth. This planet takes nearly 2 years to go around the sun. The Viking spacecraft that landed on Mars sent pictures of the planet back to earth. They show that Mars is rough and rocky, like our

Mars looks much like earth's moon.

moon. Scientists say that life is possible on Mars, but life has not yet been found there. Mars has 2 tiny moons, each a few miles wide.

JUPITER is the giant of the solar system. It is about 11 times as wide as the earth. It is so big that more than a thousand earths could be packed into it. Temperatures on Jupiter are hundreds

Jupiter is bigger than a thousand earths.

of degrees below zero. Jupiter takes almost 12 years to make a trip around the sun. This planet has 16 moons. It also has a set of rings around it, which are too thin to be seen from earth.

SATURN is nearly 10 times as wide as the earth. This planet takes almost 30 years to go once around the sun. Saturn has a set of huge, flat rings around it.

Rocks, ice, and dust make up the rings around Saturn.

The rings are made of rocks, ice, and dust. Besides the rings, there are 22 moons going around Saturn. On this planet, it is even colder than on Jupiter.

URANUS is almost 4 times as wide as the earth. It takes 84 years to go around the sun. This planet is even colder than Saturn. There is a set of rings around Uranus, but they are too thin to be seen. Uranus has 5 moons.

NEPTUNE is also nearly 4 times as wide as the earth. It is just a little wider than Uranus. Neptune takes 165 years to make a trip around the sun. This planet is even colder than Uranus. Neptune has 2 moons.

PLUTO is the smallest of all the planets. It is even smaller than our moon. Pluto takes 250 years to make one trip around the sun. Pluto is very cold because it is so very far away from the sun. From Pluto, the sun would look as small as a star. Pluto has one tiny moon about 750 miles (1,200 kilometers) wide.

The Sun

On a clear night there are many things to see in the sky. There are twinkling stars, bright planets, and often a silvery moon. But on a clear day, there is just one main thing that shows itself in the sky. And that is the one you know best of all. It is the sun.

How well you know the sun! It rises every morning to start a new day. It makes beautiful colors in the sky when it sets in the evening. The sun warms the earth. Its light makes everything bright and cheerful.

You must never look straight at the sun. It is much too bright. It is so bright that it can do great harm to your eyes if you look at it.

The sun is a ball. It is so huge that more than a hundred earths could fit across it, side by side. But the sun does not seem that big to us here on earth. That is because it is so far away.

The sun is very bright and very hot. But it is not on fire. You know that a burning piece of wood is hot and bright. Soon it burns up and is gone. But the sun is not burning in the same way that wood burns. Instead, the sun glows.

Anything that glows sends out light and heat from itself. For example, the tiny wire inside an electric light bulb glows. You can see the bright light it sends out. You can feel the heat if you hold your hand near the bulb. But the wire does not burn. If it did, it would be gone very quickly. It only glows.

Wood burns up, but the sun does not.

The sun glows hotter and brighter than a million H-bombs, all exploding at the same time. The sun is so hot that nothing can be solid there, not even iron. The great heat makes iron float around like a cloud of steam.

Scientists can take movies of the sun with special cameras. These movies show that huge, bright flares blast out from the sun. Flares are clouds of hot gas. They go a thousand times faster than a bullet. Some of them shoot out many thousands of miles.

The sun turns on its axis, just as the planets do. But it takes nearly a month to make one full turn. Sometimes there are dark patches on the sun. They are carried along as the sun turns. These patches are not as hot and bright as the sun itself. They are huge whirlpools of gas called sunspots.

A light bulb glows. So does the sun.

All around the sun there is a silvery glow called the corona. It is a thin cloud of very hot gas that stretches outward for millions of miles. Most of the time you cannot see the corona because the sun itself is so bright. But there are times when our moon passes exactly in front of the sun and hides it for a short time. This is called an eclipse of the sun. Then, if you are at the right place on the earth, you will be able to see the corona.

Bright flares shoot out from the sun, and all around is the silvery corona. The dark patches on the sun are sunspots.

What Is a Star?

Scientists who study the sky are called astronomers. They learn many things about the sun, the planets, and the faraway stars.

A long time ago, astronomers found that they could use glass lenses and mirrors to build telescopes. A telescope can make things look much nearer and clearer than before. With a telescope, astronomers can see the craters on the moon. They can see the rings of Saturn. They can see the moons of Jupiter. Sometime, if you get a chance to look through a big telescope, you will see all these things yourself.

When you see a star through a telescope, it does not look nearer at all. It still looks only like a tiny, sparkling dot. The stars are so very far away that even a telescope cannot make them seem bigger.

But a telescope lets you see many more stars than you could see before. It helps you see stars that are much too dim to see with your eyes alone. Astronomers know that there are billions of billions of stars in the sky! Without telescopes, you can see only a few thousand.

There is a good chance that other stars have planets moving around them. But these planets would be too dim and far away to show up in a telescope.

How can astronomers find out anything about a star if it is only a dot in a telescope? They hook up cameras and special instruments to the telescope. With these instruments, they can find out many things from the light of a star.

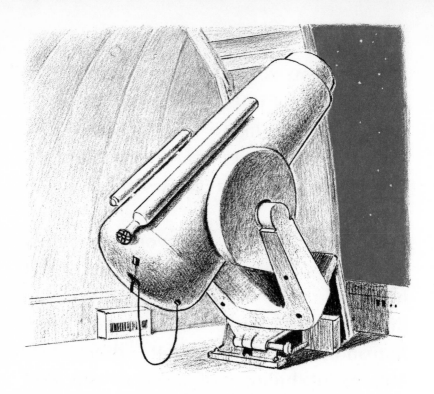

Astronomers use telescopes with special instruments to study light from the stars.

The rays of light can show how big a star is and what it is made of. They tell how far away a star is, and how it is moving. They can even tell how hot a star is.

Astronomers know that stars are hot and glowing, like our sun. The sun is just a star that happens to be near us. That is why it looks like a huge, glowing ball. All the other stars are very much farther away from us. So they seem to be only tiny dots.

There are giant stars and dwarf stars. Some giant stars are so big that our sun would be only a little speck next to one of them. And some dwarf stars are much smaller than our earth.

Astronomers find out all these things from the weak stream of light that comes from a faraway star. They can do this without ever being able to get near any star. It would take thousands and thousands of years to get to the nearest star in a fast spaceship.

Some giant stars are many times as big as our sun.

GIANT STAR

SUN

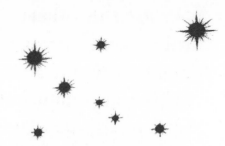

Changes in the Sky

People say that the stars "come out" at night. But the stars really do not come out at all. They are there all the time. The stars are always in the sky, night and day. But you cannot see them in the daytime because the sky is too bright. After the sun sets and the sky gets dark, you are able to see many stars.

All the stars seem to move slowly across the sky. You cannot really see this movement because it happens so slowly. It is like watching the hour hand of a clock. You know the hand moves, but you cannot see it moving.

44

You can prove that the stars are always changing their place in the sky. Early some evening, go outdoors and face toward the south. Choose any bright star. Then move around a little until you can see this star just above a house or near a post. Mark the place where you stand.

Go outdoors again about an hour later. Stand in the very same spot as

You can prove that the stars seem to move across the sky.

before. Now you see your star in a different place in the sky. You find it a little farther west than it was at first. And all the other stars seem to have moved toward the west along with it.

But the stars are not moving along at all. It is really the earth that moves. The earth turns on its axis. And this turning makes the stars seem to go from east to west across the sky.

It is like riding on a merry-go-round. The people who are watching seem to be moving past you. But they are standing still. You are the one who is going around.

That is how it is with the stars. The earth turns, and you turn with it. And it seems as if you are not moving, while the stars are going past you.

Find Some Stars

Long, long ago, people knew very little about stars. But the stars helped them in many ways. People learned to tell time by the stars. They marked the seasons of the year that way, too. The stars took the place of a clock and a calendar.

In the old days, people wondered about the stars as they looked up at the night sky. They thought the groups of stars made pictures in the sky, and they gave each group a name.

One set of stars seemed to look like a bear. The drawing on the next page shows why this group got the name Great Bear.

This star group is called the Great Bear. The Big
Dipper is part of the group.

In the Great Bear, there is a set of
seven bright stars. This set is called the
Big Dipper, and you can see why. It
looks like a cup with a long handle. This
kind of cup is called a dipper.

There are many other star groups in
the sky. You see different groups at different times because the earth keeps
turning.

Go hunting for stars on any clear night. Some of the groups are easy to find. You can see the Big Dipper best in summer. Face north. Look high in the sky. And there it is.

The Big Dipper is harder to see in winter. At that time it is lower in the sky. Then part of it may be hidden if there are hills or tall buildings near you.

Now find the North Star. This star is also called the Pole Star because it is above the North Pole of the earth.

Use the Big Dipper to help find the North Star. First look at the picture on the next page. Notice the line through the two outside stars of the cup. This line points to the North Star. Now, look at the sky and imagine the same line in the Big Dipper. It will lead you to the North Star.

You always see the North Star in about the same place in the sky. That is because it happens to be along the earth's axis, above the North Pole.

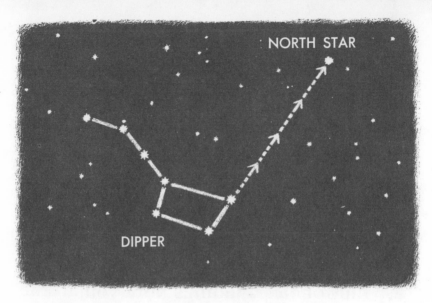

The Big Dipper points to the North Star.

Long ago, sailors used the North Star to find their way at sea. They knew that this star always held its place in the north, while all the others kept moving across the sky. The captain of a ship in the middle of the ocean could trust the North Star to point the way.

Look for a star group called Orion. You will know it from the picture on the next page. A very long time ago, there was a story about a giant hunter named Orion. People thought this group of stars looked like him. It seemed to them that the bright star near the top was the shoulder of the hunter. One of the lower stars was his knee. His belt was the row of three stars.

Winter is the best time of year to find Orion. Face south and look high in the sky. First of all, find the three stars in a row. Then it will be easy to pick out the top and bottom stars. Notice that the top star looks reddish and the bottom star looks bluish.

This star group is called Orion.

A Band of Stars

Look up at the sky some night in fall when it is quite dark. Be sure to do it when there are no clouds in the sky and the moon is not up.

At first you can see only a few bright stars. Then, as your eyes get used to the darkness, you see more and more stars. After a while, the dark sky seems to be full of sparkling stars wherever you look. There are reddish stars, bluish stars, white stars. There are bright glittery ones. And some stars are so dim, you can hardly be sure you see them at all.

Now look high overhead. Do you see a

wide path of pale whiteness all across the sky? It looks almost like a stretched-out band of thin clouds. But this band is really made up of stars. There are billions of them! There are so many that you cannot see each star by itself. Instead, there seems to be a path of lightness across the dark sky. This white band is called the Milky Way.

The Milky Way is made up of a huge number of stars that stay together in space. Our sun is just one of the billions of stars in it. This kind of group is called a galaxy. There are billions of other galaxies spread all through space.

The Milky Way is part of our galaxy.

Some Strange Things in Space

QUASARS

Telescopes that pick up light from the stars were invented almost 400 years ago. Less than 50 years ago, another kind of telescope was invented. It is called a radio telescope.

Instead of collecting waves of light, radio telescopes pick up radio waves. If you have a radio at home, you can pick up the radio waves sent out by broadcasting stations on earth. Most of the waves picked up by radio telescopes come from the sun and from some of the other stars.

Radio telescopes are also picking up something new and surprising. They are bringing in radio waves that are billions of times as strong as the waves from an ordinary star. These unusual waves come from places that are very, very far out in space.

Anything that sends out such strong radio waves is called a quasar. No ordinary star could send out waves of this much power. Up to now, astronomers have not been able to find out what these mysterious quasars really are.

A radio telescope picks up radio waves from outer space.

A few years ago, radio telescopes began to pick up sudden bursts of radio waves from outer space. The bursts are very evenly timed, coming about a second apart. Anything in space that sends out such bursts of radio waves is called a pulsar.

Pulsars must be quite small. Otherwise, their flashes of radio waves could not be so sharp. Astronomers believe that a pulsar starts out as a large star. Then it shrinks down until it is only about 10 miles (16 kilometers) across. That would be like squeezing a huge mountain down to the size of a marble.

What could make a pulsar flash on and off in such a steady way? There may be "hot spots" on it. As the pulsar spins, the beam of radio waves from a hot spot swings around through space. Sometimes the earth is in the path of one of these beams. Then, as the beam of radio waves sweeps across the earth, it is picked up by radio telescopes. This happens again and again as the pulsar spins.

BLACK HOLES

Quasars and pulsars are a great puzzle to astronomers. But there may be other things in space that are even more mysterious.

It is possible that a star might squeeze down until it is even smaller than a pulsar. The pull of gravity near this kind of star would be so strong that nothing could escape from it. Not even light could get away. A beam of light or a cloud of gas that started out would be sucked back into the star.

So, if no light could get away, the star could not be seen from the outside. It would be just a "black hole" in space!

How Big Is Space?

Now you can begin to think about the bigness of outer space.

Start with the sun. It would take almost a year to get there by spaceship. How far away from us the sun is!

But the sun is only our nearest star. Some of the other stars in our galaxy are billions of times farther away.

And that is not all. There are billions of galaxies spread through space, each one far from its nearest neighbor.

All of outer space, with everything in it, has a name. It is called the universe.

There is much more in the universe than astronomers have been able to discover with their telescopes. They believe there are more stars, more galaxies, and much more space.

And they will keep on trying, always, to find out as much as they can about the wonders of the universe.

Many galaxies have a pin-wheel shape like this one.

Index